CHIRPING INSECTS

CHIRPING INSECTS

by Sylvia A. Johnson

Photographs by Yuko Sato

A Lerner Natural Science Book

Lerner Publications Company ▪ Minneapolis

Sylvia A. Johnson, Series Editor

Translation of original text by Phyllis Hyland Larson.

The publisher wishes to thank Jerry W. Heaps, Entomologist, for his assistance in the preparation of this book.

Photograph on page 22 by Joanne Pavia, Kaleidoscope.
Drawing on page 25 by Yoshitaka Moriue.

A note on the classification of chirping insects appears on page 45. The glossary on page 46 gives definitions and pronunciations of words shown in **bold type** in the text.

LIBRARY OF CONGRESS CATALOGING-IN-PUBLICATION DATA

Johnson, Sylvia A.
  Chirping insects.

  (A Lerner natural science book)
  Adaptation of: Naku mushi no sekai / by Oda, Hidetomo.
  Includes index.
  Summary: Describes how chirping insects such as crickets, katydids, and grasshoppers produce their songs and use them to send messages to other members of their species.
  1. Orthoptera—Juvenile literature. 2. Insects—Juvenile literature. [1. Crickets. 2. Grasshoppers. 3. Cicada. 4. Insects] I. Satō, Yūko, 1928-   ill. II. Oda, Hidetomo. Naku mushi no sekai. III. Title. IV. Series.
  QL506.J65   1986   595.7'260459   86-15380
  ISBN 0-8225-1486-9 (lib. bdg.)

International Standard Book Number: 0-8225-1486-9
Library of Congress Catalog Card Number: 86-15380

    2 3 4 5 6 7 8 9 10 96 95 94 93 92 91 90 89 88 87

Through the warm air of a late summer night comes a chorus of harsh and monotonous noises. It sounds as if thousands of tiny saws are rasping away on dry wood. The noises rise from the fields and the dark woods, filling the night with a strange and haunting music.

The mysterious sounds are made by insects that are among the most accomplished "singers" of the animal world. This book describes some of these chirping insects and the varied ways in which they produce their remarkable sounds.

MEET THE ORTHOPTERANS

Most of the insects whose chirping is heard on summer nights are members of the scientific order called **Orthoptera**. This is a very large group made up of around 20,000 different species that live in most parts of the world. Among the orthopterans are such familiar insects as grasshoppers, crickets, and katydids.

The word *Orthoptera* means "straight-winged," which describes one of the characteristic traits of the order: long, straight front wings. The numerous orthopterans are further divided into two suborders, each of which has slightly different physical features. The most conspicuous is the difference in the length of the **antennae**, or feelers, that the insects bear on their heads.

Members of the suborder **Caelifera**, which includes many kinds of grasshoppers, have short antennae. The insects in the suborder **Ensifera**—among them crickets and katydids—often have antennae longer than their bodies.

The names of scientific groups such as Caelifera and Ensifera may be difficult to pronounce and remember, but they are very important in talking about insects like the ones described in this book. The common names of the orthopterans—grasshopper, katydid, cricket—are often used in a confusing and unclear manner. In order to identify the insects correctly, scientists usually refer to them by their scientific names and groups as well as their common names. You will find this system of naming used in the following pages.

Shown here are three of the
chirping insects in the order
Orthoptera. Above right: This
short-horned grasshopper belongs to the suborder Caelifera.
Its common name refers to the
short antennae typical of the
group. Below: Both of these
long-antennaed insects are
members of the suborder Ensifera. On the left is a long-
horned grasshopper and, on
the right, a cricket.

Its long hind legs trailing behind, an orthopteran glides through the air on its two pairs of wings.

Although the different groups of orthopterans have antennae of varying lengths and differ in other ways, most have the straight front wings that gives their order its name. These unusual front wings, called **tegmina**, are often thick and leathery. The hind wings, on the other hand, are broad and filmy, as you can see in the photograph above.

When an orthopteran flies, it uses both pairs of wings, although the wide hind wings do most of the work. Actually, the insects in this order are not very good fliers, compared to houseflies, dragonflies, and other skilled insect aerialists. Many orthopterans spend most of their time on the ground or in trees and shrubs. Some members of the order have very tiny wings or no wings at all and are incapable of flight.

This young short-horned grasshopper has the powerful jumping legs of all members of the order Orthoptera.

What the orthopterans lack in flying ability, they make up for in their talent for jumping. Grasshoppers and other insects in this order are capable of jumps as long as three feet (1 meter). These amazing leaps are powered by the insects' long, heavy hind legs. An orthopteran's hind legs are much larger than the other two pairs, and they usually stick up high above the body when the insect is on the ground. The numerous muscles in these powerful legs enable an orthopteran to propel itself into the air with great ease.

These tiny, fragile creatures are nymphs, the immature form of orthopteran insects. The cricket nymph on the left has just emerged from an egg buried in the soil. On the opposite page is another orthopteran nymph that has already developed the large hind legs of an adult.

Another characteristic shared by all members of the order Orthoptera is the way in which the insects develop into adults. In contrast to the four-stage development of insects such as butterflies, beetles, and bees, orthopterans go through a three-stage process known as **incomplete metamorphosis**.

During the four stages of **complete metamorphosis**, a butterfly experiences several changes in form. It hatches from its egg as a worm-like larva and then develops into a pupa hidden inside a protective covering. After another change in form, the adult butterfly emerges from the pupal covering.

The changes that take place during the three stages of incomplete metamorphosis are much less drastic than the ones that produce a butterfly. Orthopterans and other insects such as dragonflies emerge from their eggs not as larvae but as **nymphs**. Nymphs look much like the adults of their species, except that they are smaller and lacking in some adult body parts. As a nymph grows, these parts gradually develop and the insect becomes a full-fledged adult.

Nymphs feeding on parts of dandelion flowers. Like adult orthopterans, nymphs eat leaves, flowers, and seeds of green plants. A few members of the group also eat insects, including members of their own species.

Holding onto a plant leaf with its sharp claws, a molting nymph pulls itself out of its old skin. At this point in its development, its wings are very small.

On its way to becoming an adult, an orthopteran nymph goes through several different stages of growth. Like all insects, a nymph is covered by an **exoskeleton** made up of hard material that does not expand as its body grows larger. In order to increase in size, the nymph must **molt**, or shed, its exoskeleton.

Most orthopteran nymphs molt at least four times during their development. A nymph hangs by its feet from a leaf or twig and twists its body until a split develops in the old exoskeleton. The insect pulls itself out through the opening, leaving the old covering hanging from the leaf. Its

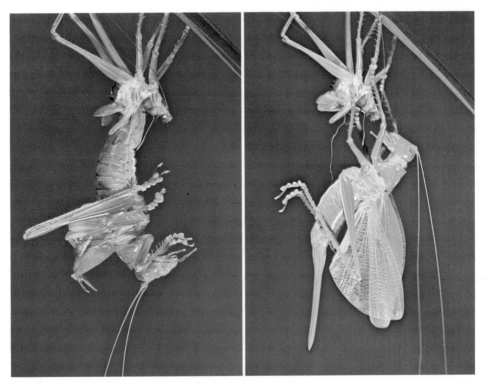

The final molt reveals a completely developed adult insect, with full-sized wings. The long antennae of this newly emerged orthopteran indicates that it is a member of the suborder Ensifera.

body is protected by a new exoskeleton that allows room for growth. This covering is soft at first, but after being exposed to the air, it hardens.

As a nymph goes through its various molts, its wings gradually develop from little knobs or pads into their full size. At the final molt, the insect emerges from the old exoskeleton as a completely developed adult, with all the body parts needed to live an adult life.

This short-horned grasshopper belongs to the family Acrididae and the genus *Parapodisma*. It has very small wings and does not produce sound like many of its relatives.

CAELIFERA: THE SHORT-HORNED GRASSHOPPERS

Now that we have found out about the general characteristics of the orthopterans, it's time to meet some individual members of this large order. Let's start with representatives of the suborder Caelifera.

The insects in this group all have short antennae, as you will remember, and they also share another important characteristic that makes them easy to identify. This is the shape of the **ovipositor**, the tube at the end of a female insect's abdomen through which eggs are laid. Members of Caelifera have a blunt, chisel-shaped ovipositor, in contrast to the slender, sword-like ovipositor of the orthopterans in the other suborder, Ensifera. In fact, the scientific names of the two groups are based on this difference; *Caelifera* means "chisel-bearer," while *Ensifera* means "sword-bearer."

The most familiar of the "chisel-bearing" orthopterans are the lively, leaping insects commonly known as short-horned grasshoppers. They belong to one of the subdivisions of Caelifera, the family **Acrididae**.

 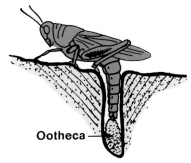

Ootheca —

This photograph illustrates the way in which female short-horned grasshoppers use their chisel-shaped ovipositors in laying eggs. After a female mates with a male of her species, she digs a hole in loose soil with her blunt, powerful ovipositor. Then she extends her abdomen down into the hole and lays the eggs that have developed inside her body. The eggs are enclosed in a case, or ootheca, made of a foamy material that hardens and provides protection. Short-horned grasshopper eggs are often laid in the autumn and hatch the following spring.

17

This short-horned grasshopper *(Chorthippus latippenis)* is stridu-lating by rubbing one of its hind legs against a front wing.

Short-horned grasshoppers are found in many parts of the world, living in meadows and fields and feeding on plant material. Although not all of the insects produce sound, many are accomplished musicians, filling the warm summer air with their rasping songs.

Like all the chirping orthopterans, short-horned grass-hoppers lack vocal chords and other structures possessed by true singing animals like birds and humans. Instead, they make sounds by rubbing together parts of their bodies. The scientific name for this method of sound production is called **stridulation**.

An enlarged photograph of the file-like structure on a short-horned grasshopper's hind leg

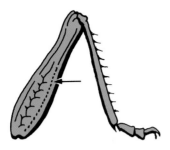

Orthopterans (usually only the males) stridulate in several different ways. Most short-horned grasshoppers rub their hind legs against their front wings. On the inside of the femur, or lower section, of each hind leg is a file-like structure composed of many tiny teeth. When this file is rubbed against a ridge on the insect's front wing, it sets up vibrations that are heard as sounds.

The tympanum, or hearing organ, of a short-horned grasshopper

Orthopterans do not have the complicated ears of mammals, but they do have an organ capable of "hearing" the sounds of stridulation. This organ, known as a **tympanum** (plural, **tympana**), is a tightly stretched membrane that, like a human eardrum, responds to vibrations.

The tympana of the various orthopterans are located in different areas of the body. Short-horned grasshoppers, like most members of the suborder Caelifera, have these membranes on either side of their abdomens, just above their hind legs.

Each kind of orthopteran seems to have tympana especially tuned to the vibrations produced by other members of the same species. Although many orthopterans may be singing at the same time in the same area, the individual songs are probably music only to the ears of the singers' close relatives.

This orthopteran is a member of the large family Tettigoniidae.

ENSIFERA: THE TETTIGONIIDS

The suborder Ensifera includes some of the noisiest and most varied of the orthopterans. All of these insects are noted for their long antennae, and the females in the group have the slender, sword-like ovipositor that has given the suborder its name.

Like Caelifera, the suborder Ensifera is divided into several large families of insects. One of the most important is the family **Tettigoniidae**. There is not much agreement about the common names of the insects in this group, which is found in most parts of the world. In English-speaking countries like the United States, many members of the family Tettigoniidae are known as long-horned grasshoppers, while some are called katydids. Other English-speaking people refer to the insects as bush crickets. To avoid such confusion, we will use the word *tettigoniid* for all the members of this varied family.

21

The photographs on these two pages show two of the many kinds of tettigoniids. The graceful insect on the opposite page is a member of the genus *Phaneroptera*. It makes its home in open fields and meadows, where its long, slender body and wings resemble the narrow leaves and stems of the native plants.

Shown above is one of the tettigoniids commonly known as katydids (genus *Scudderia*). The name comes from the insects' distinctive song, which sounds like a chorus of rasping voices saying "Katy did, Katy did" over and over. This monotonous song is often heard on late summer evenings in many parts of eastern North America.

A tettigoniid produces sound by rubbing together the upper parts of its two front wings.

Tettigoniids and other members of the suborder Ensifera have their own distinctive sound-making system, different from those of the Caeliferan insects. They create their songs by rubbing together parts of their front wings, which are specially designed for this purpose.

On the underside of a tettigoniid's two front wings is a very efficient file-and-scraper device. The "file" is a row of teeth-like projections attached to a vein on the upper part of the left front wing. On the upper edge of the right wing is a ridge that serves as a scraper.

When a tettigoniid is at rest, the top of its left front wing overlaps the top of the right one, bringing the two sound-making surfaces in contact with each other. By moving its wings, the insect can rub the "file" against the "scraper," creating the chirping noises that communicate a message to other members of its species.

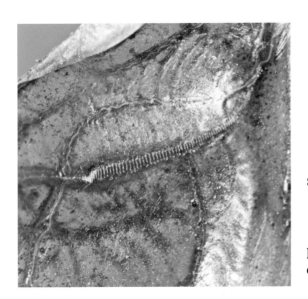

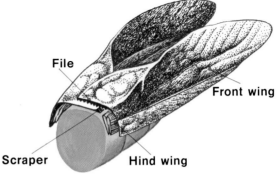

File

Front wing

Scraper

Hind wing

Left: **The "file" on the underside of a tettigoniid's left front wing**

The sound produced by a tettigoniid is magnified by a special structure called a **mirror**, located on the front wings near the file and scraper. A mirror is a circular section of wing membrane that is stretched tightly, something like the skin covering a drum. This structure picks up the vibrations created by the scraping action and amplifies them so that they carry farther.

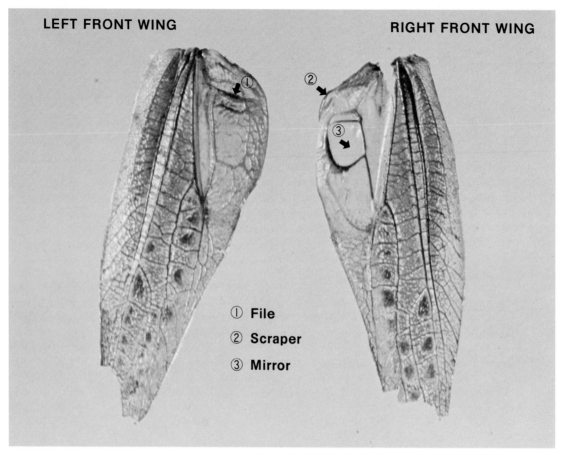

① File
② Scraper
③ Mirror

This photograph shows the two front wings of a tettigoniid and the sound-making parts that they contain.

With the help of amplification, the vibrations may eventually reach the hearing organs of another tettigoniid. These organs are located not on the insect's abdomen, as in grasshoppers, but on the lower parts of its two front legs. The tightly stretched membranes of the tympana pick up the sounds produced by other members of the same species and relay the message to the nervous system of the insect.

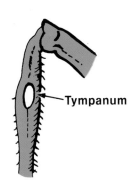

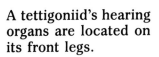

A tettigoniid's hearing organs are located on its front legs.

Most of the messages sent by tettigoniids and other orthopterans have to do with one very important subject: mating. For orthopterans as for all members of the animal world, communication is essential in finding mates and producing young. Orthopteran songs are an effective form of communication through which male insects advertise their presence and let females know that they are looking for mates.

Female orthopterans usually cannot produce sounds, but they can recognize the songs of appropriate males and use their hearing organs to locate the singers. After mating takes place, the males may resume their songs, seeking other mates. The females move on to the next stage in the process of reproduction.

27

Left: **This species of tettigon-iid, *Phaneroptera falcata*, lays its eggs inside the tissue of plant leaves.** Opposite: *Gampsocleis buergeri* deposits its eggs in loose soil.

These photographs show two female tettigoniids using their sword-like ovipositors to lay eggs. The insect in the picture above is depositing her eggs inside a plant leaf. With her body bent double, she uses the sharp point of the ovipositor to pierce the tissue of the leaf. The eggs will then pass through the hollow tube into the leaf, where they will go through their development.

The tettigoniid shown on the opposite page has an extremely long, curved ovipositor that really does resemble a sword. This insect is depositing her eggs in loose soil. Like many tettigoniids, she lays each egg separately rather than in a mass as female short-horned grasshoppers do. Tettigoniid eggs are not encased in foam like those of their distant relatives. Usually laid in late summer or autumn, they stay hidden during the winter and hatch the following spring.

Opposite and right: **These crickets (*Tereogryllus emma*) have the heavy bodies and dark coloring of many members of the family Gryllidae.**

ENSIFERA: THE CRICKETS

With their large heads and dark, heavy bodies, the crickets shown on these two pages look rather different from their slim, graceful relatives in the suborder Ensifera. Yet they have the same long antennae and sword-shaped ovipositors possessed by the tettigoniids, as well as the powerful jumping legs typical of all the orthopterans.

Most crickets belong to the family **Gryllidae**, another large subdivision of Ensifera. Although they share many habits and physical characteristics, gryllids are found in a wide variety of environments. In addition to field or ground crickets like the ones shown here, there are some gryllids that live in trees, while others make their homes in people's houses. Mole crickets, members of another cricket family, spend much of their time underground, in burrows or hollows.

These photographs of crickets in the genus *Tereogryllus* show some of the typical characteristics of most gryllids. The folded wings are held flat over the insect's back (above) rather than at the side, as among the tettigoniids. At the end of the abdomen are two long, hairy antennae known as **cerci** (right). Many crickets have these organs, which they use to find their way around in the dark. Unlike short-horned grasshoppers and some other orthopterans, most crickets are creatures of the night, remaining hidden in hollows or under vegetation during the day.

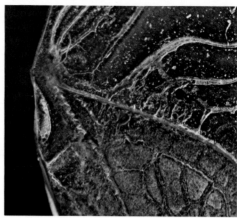

Left: **This view from behind shows a cricket stridulating with raised wings.** Above: **The file on a cricket's wing**

Of all the orthopterans, crickets are probably the best known music-makers. They are capable of singing long and loud during the dark hours of summer and early autumn nights.

The "instruments" that crickets use to stridulate are basically the same as those of the other singing Ensifera. On its front wings, a cricket has a file-and-scraper combination that produces chirps when the wings are rubbed together. In contrast to the tettigoniids, most crickets raise their wings at a 45-degree angle to their bodies when they are stridulating.

In addition to amplifying mirrors like those of the tettigoniids, crickets have another means of increasing the volume of their songs. The space between a stridulating cricket's raised wings and its body forms a kind of echo chamber that makes the chirps louder. Some crickets are able to enlarge this space and increase the echo effect by depressing their abdomens during stridulation.

Like other members of the suborder Ensifera, a cricket has a tympanum on each of its two front legs (below). By means of these hearing organs, the insect can pick up the sounds produced by other members of its species and respond to the messages they convey.

A male cricket (right) sings to attract an approaching female (left).

When a cricket produces its chirping song, the message being sent is usually an invitation to meet and mate. Male crickets are the message-senders, and they are broadcasting their plea to females of their particular species.

When a female hears an appropriate mating song, she moves in the direction of the singer, using the "ears" on her legs to track the direction from which the sound is coming. The male usually stays in one place and continues to broadcast until the female finds him. Then he may change his tune to a "courtship song" designed to persuade the female to accept him as a mate.

Two crickets mating. The female is on top of the male.

Among crickets and other male orthopterans, chirping can also be used as a means of establishing superiority over other males of the same species. Sometimes two males will have a singing contest, answering each other chirp for chirp. At other times, a male orthopteran may use his music to claim a particular territory as his own. All these songs are different, usually varying in the number of chirps and the time intervals between them.

With wings raised high, a tree cricket (genus *Ornebius)* chirps its sweet song.

Tree crickets are members of the family Gryllidae, but they look very different from most of their dark, thick-bodied relatives. These graceful gryllids are usually pale in color and have long, thin bodies. Despite their common name, not all tree crickets live in trees. Many spend their time hidden in bushes or other kinds of thick vegetation.

From their leafy perches, tree crickets sing songs that are noted for their high pitch and clear, sweet sound. Some of these gryllid serenades are famous as a source of information about the weather. Several species of tree crickets in the genus *Oecanthus* are popularly known as thermometer

These two tree crickets are members of the genus *Oecanthus*, which is common in many parts of the world.

crickets because the frequency of their chirps is supposed to indicate the temperature. (The usual formula is the number of chirps in 15 seconds plus 39 equals the temperature in degrees Fahrenheit.)

The tree cricket's reputation as a weather indicator may be exaggerated, but it is based on scientific fact. The frequency of an orthopteran's stridulations does seem to be influenced by environmental conditions, especially temperature. Studies have shown that insects singing during the day will change the rate of their chirps when a cloud passes overhead, causing the temperature to drop.

Opposite: **Like orthopterans, cicadas develop through incomplete metamorphosis. This photograph shows an adult cicada emerging after its final molt.**

THE CICADA: A DIFFERENT DRUMMER

The orthopterans are the best known sound-makers in the insect world, but there is one other noteworthy musician that belongs to a different insect order. This is the **cicada**, a member of the order Homoptera.

Cicadas are capable of producing a great deal of noise, but they are not stridulators like the orthopterans. Instead of rubbing parts of their bodies together, male cicadas use their muscles to vibrate drum-like membranes in their abdomens. These membranes, called **timbals**, are located inside resonating cavities that increase the volume of the sound.

The cicada's harsh song, like the more musical outpourings of the orthopterans, is used to attract a mate. Male cicadas, however, are not as competitive as their distant relatives. Large numbers of the insects will often gather together in trees and sing, combining their sounds into a loud, buzzing chorus that can be heard from far away. A female attracted by the noise selects an individual male, who then serenades her with a courtship song.

This species of cricket, *Homoeogryllus japonicus*, lives in Japan. Because it has a very clear, bell-like chirp, it is commonly known as the bell-ring insect.

A male tree cricket (genus *Ornebius*) walking along the branch of a tree

CHIRPING INSECTS

Most insects have never been very popular among people, but the chirping insects have always had a special place in the human world. In China, Japan, and other Asian countries, the songs of crickets are appreciated so much that caged crickets are often kept as pets in the same way that others keep song birds. For people in many parts of the world, the chirping of crickets and other orthopterans is a memorable sound of late summer, a reminder that the warm days and nights will soon give way to the cool weather of autumn.

The music of the chirping orthopterans seems to carry a message not only to the insects but also to listening humans.

SORTING OUT THE ORDER ORTHOPTERA

The scientific order Orthoptera is a complex group made up of approximately 20,000 different species, or kinds, of insects. In order to understand the relationships among these thousands of creatures, scientists have broken the order down into smaller groupings.

There are two *suborders* of Orthoptera, each consisting of many insect *families.* (Some scientists place a *superfamily* grouping between these two levels of classification.) Families are divided into *genera* (singular, *genus*), and each genus is made up of one or more *species.*

Following is a list of the main orthopteran groups mentioned in this book:

CAELIFERA

Family Acrididae
Parapodisma
Chorthippus

ENSIFERA

Family Tettigoniidae
Scudderia
Phaneroptera
Gampsocleis

Family Gryllidae
Tereogryllus
Ornebius
Oecanthus
Homoeogryllus

GLOSSARY

Acrididae (eh-KRID-ih-dee)—a family of orthopterans that includes short-horned grasshoppers

antennae (an-TEN-ee)—sense organs on the heads of insects that respond to vibrations and odors

Caelifera (suh-LIF-uhr-uh)—one of the two suborders of Orthoptera, made up of short-horned grasshoppers and other insects with short antennae and chisel-shaped ovipositors

cerci (SURH-see)—feelers on the abdomens of some orthopterans. The singular form of the word is **cercus (SUHR-kuhs)**.

cicada (sih-KAY-duh)—an insect that produces sound by vibrating membranes on its abdomen. Cicadas are members of the scientific order Homoptera.

Ensifera (en-SIF-uhr-uh)—one of the two suborders of Orthoptera, made up of crickets, long-horned grasshoppers, and other insects with long antennae and sword-shaped ovipositors

exoskeleton—the tough outer covering of an insect's body that protects the internal organs and provides a framework for muscles

Gryllidae (GRIL-ih-dee)—a family of orthopterans that includes crickets

metamorphosis (met-uh-MOR-fuh-sis)—the process of growth that produces most adult insects. Grasshoppers, crickets, and other orthopterans go through a gradual three-stage development known as **incomplete metamorphosis;** the three stages are egg, nymph, and adult. **Complete meta-**

morphosis has four stages: egg, larva, pupa, and adult. Bees, butterflies, ants, and many other kinds of insects develop by this process.

mirror—a section of an orthopteran's front wing that amplifies the sounds produced by stridulation

molt—to shed the outer covering of the body

nymphs (NIMFS)—the immature forms of orthopterans and other insects that develop through incomplete metamorphosis. Nymphs look like small versions of adults, lacking only a few body parts.

ootheca (oo-THEE-kuh)—a case made from a foamy material that encloses the eggs of some female orthopterans

Orthoptera (or-THAHP-teh-ruh)—the scientific order that includes grasshoppers, crickets, and other chirping insects

ovipositor (oh-vee-POS-ih-tur)—the tube at the end of a female insect's abdomen through which eggs leave the body

stridulation (strij-uh-LAY-shun)—a method of producing sounds by rubbing two body parts together

tegmina (TEG-mih-nuh)—the front wings of orthopterans, often used in sound production. The singular form of the word is **tegmen**.

Tettigoniidae (ted-ih-GON-ee-ih-dee)—a family of orthopterans that includes the insects commonly known as katydids and long-horned grasshoppers

timbals (TIM-buhls)—drum-like membranes on the abdomens of cicadas used to produce sound

tympanum (TIM-pih-nuhm)—a tightly stretched membrane that serves as a sound receptor.

INDEX